Whispers of the Forgotten

Introduction:

They told me history was already written, neatly archived, catalogued, and cross-checked by those more qualified than me. Professors pointed to textbooks, historians cited peer-reviewed papers, and archaeologists gestured to carefully curated museum exhibits. The past, they assured me, had been thoroughly examined and properly explained. Yet with each passing year, their explanations felt increasingly hollow—like a stage play where the props wobble if you stare too long. The more I learned about "official" history, the more I sensed the presence of something vast lurking just beyond the edges of our collective awareness.

But something deep inside whispered, even screamed at times, that we had missed something. It wasn't just a hunch or a passing curiosity—it was an insistent, gnawing feeling that the world we live in is built upon layers of forgotten truth. I began noticing anomalies everywhere: buildings that made no sense within their supposed time periods, technologies that appeared too advanced for their eras, and entire cultures that seemed to emerge fully formed without any clear origin. The deeper I looked, the more the cracks in the mainstream narrative widened.

Not just a minor detail or forgotten figure, but an entire civilization. Not merely a footnote lost to time, but a global super-culture that once thrived and was then systematically erased. I'm talking about Tartaria—or whatever name it truly carried before history was rewritten. The evidence is scattered but undeniable: in the phantom traces of star forts, in the eerie similarities between distant megalithic structures, in the inexplicable prevalence of orphan trains and reset narratives across multiple continents. This was not a small oversight. This was a deliberate burial.

A paradigm-shifting truth buried beneath centuries of misinformation and cognitive dissonance. The more I uncovered, the more I realized how deeply the deception ran. It wasn't just a matter of lost records or accidental omissions. There were forces—whether by design or by the inertia of institutionalized dogma—that actively suppressed this knowledge. The mainstream gatekeepers of history dismissed anomalies as coincidences, labelled dissenting researchers as conspiracy theorists, and mocked anyone who dared question the established timeline. But the truth has a way of resurfacing, no matter how thoroughly it's suppressed.

Whispers of the Forgotten Empire

I'm not a scholar, not an archaeologist, nor a time-traveling sage. I don't have a PhD, and I've never set foot in a prestigious university's archives. But perhaps that's why I was able to see what the experts missed. Unburdened by academic dogma, I followed the breadcrumbs wherever they led—through old maps, suppressed patents, bizarre world's fair exhibitions, and the haunting accounts of those who remembered things that "never happened." The deeper I went, the clearer it became: we are living inside a story that has been heavily edited.

I'm just a soul who couldn't let the whispers fade. And those whispers came from everywhere—from the strange symbols hidden in plain sight on banknotes, from the cryptic admissions of 19th-century Freemasons, from the orphaned children who were shipped across continents with no explanation. The more I listened, the louder

Whispers of the Forgotten Empire

the whispers grew, until they became a chorus of voices from a forgotten past, crying out to be remembered.

This book is not a thesis or an argument. I'm not here to convince the sceptics or debate the academics. This is a record of my journey—a trail of clues, dead ends, sudden breakthroughs, and moments of sheer awe as the puzzle pieces began to fit together. Some of what you'll read may sound unbelievable. Some of it may resonate in ways you can't yet explain. That's okay. Truth doesn't need to be defended; it just needs to be seen.

It's my journey. A mosaic of revelations, questions, synchronicities, and wild, wonderful theories that somehow feel more real than the narrative we've been handed. Along the way, I've met others who've seen the same patterns—architects baffled by "impossible" construction techniques, genealogists who can't trace lineages past a certain date, and everyday people who've experienced glitches in the fabric of reality itself. This isn't just about Tartaria. It's about the nature of history, memory, and the stories we tell ourselves to make sense of the world.

I am a Tartarianist. That doesn't mean I have all the answers. It means I've chosen to question everything. To look at the world not as it's presented, but as it truly might be—a palimpsest of lost empires, hidden technologies, and rewritten chronologies. Being a Tartarianist isn't about proving a theory; it's about awakening to the possibility that our past is far stranger, grander, and more mysterious than we've been led to believe.

This is my story. But it might also be yours. Because if even a fraction of what I've uncovered is true, then we are all living in the aftermath of something extraordinary—something that was taken from us. And if that's the case, then remembering isn't just an intellectual exercise. It's an act of reclamation.

Welcome to the path less travelled.
Welcome to Tartaria.

Chapter 1: The Awakening

It all started with a photograph; not a relic or an ancient map, just a photo I saw on a social media feed. It was one of those grand, ornate buildings with impossibly intricate domes, columns, and statues. The caption read: "Built in 1889."

I remember staring at it, confused. 1889? It looked like something from ancient Rome or a fairy-tale kingdom. I'd seen cathedrals and government buildings before, but this one was different; not just because of its size or beauty, but because something in me instantly rejected the date. It felt like a lie.

From that moment, my perception began to crack. I dove into old images, blueprints, maps, and engravings. What I found was a strange pattern: hundreds, maybe thousands, of structures across the world that shared the same style. Monolithic buildings with technology that shouldn't have existed when they were supposedly built. Entire world fairs constructed with impossible speed, then demolished just as quickly. Who builds something so magnificent, only to tear it down a few years later?

The inconsistencies began piling up. The deeper I went, the more questions arose. Why did so many buildings from the late 1800s look ancient? Why did cities like Chicago, San Francisco, and St. Louis have massive architectural projects right before mysterious fires, floods, or earthquakes destroyed them? Why were there mudfloods in places that weren't prone to them?

Then I stumbled across the term: Tartaria. It felt like a missing puzzle piece I didn't even know I was searching for; a supposed empire, sprawling and advanced, wiped from mainstream history. They said it was just a myth. I didn't believe them.

The more I looked, the more I found. And the more I found, the more I realized this wasn't about proving something to anyone else; it was about waking up to a reality that had been hidden in plain sight.

The world changed for me that day. It wasn't a lightning bolt or a grand epiphany. It was quieter—subtler. Like a veil had lifted. I didn't choose to become a Tartarianist; I was called into it. And once you see, you can't unsee.

That first photograph became the gateway. I started saving others—images of structures I'd never noticed before. Train stations that looked like cathedrals. Courthouses with golden domes. Libraries so vast and ornate, they could have been palaces. It was as if there had been another layer to reality just waiting for me to notice. A kind of architectural deja vu that whispered, "This wasn't built for you... this was inherited."

I started visiting some of these buildings in person. I'd walk their halls, feel the cold stone beneath my hands, listen for the echo of something ancient. And there was always that feeling—like the structure was watching me back. Like it remembered something I had forgotten.

At night, I'd lie awake thinking about what we've lost—or rather, what we've been made to forget. What if we didn't evolve to where we are now, but instead fell from something higher? What if the world we're living in isn't the first version, but a pale copy built over the ruins of a far more advanced civilization?

This journey hasn't just been about history or architecture. It's been about waking up. About remembering. About recognizing that something deep within me has always known the story we've been told isn't the whole truth.

This is not just a retelling of facts—it's an emotional, spiritual, and intellectual reckoning with the world I thought I knew. And it all began with a single photograph; one small image that cracked open a doorway into a forgotten empire.

I didn't set out to become a seeker. But once you hear the whispers of the forgotten, they never truly leave you.

Whispers of the Forgotten Empire

And so, I followed them.

Chapter 2: The Cracks in the Foundation

I suppose I always knew something didn't quite add up. The world around me—its history, its monuments, the sheer arrogance with which our reality was packaged and delivered—never quite sat right. As a child, I'd ask questions that were met with gentle shrugs or impatient redirections. "That's just how it is," they'd say, or "Don't worry about it, you'll understand when you're older." But the answers never came. Instead, the questions just got louder.

It started with buildings, strangely enough. Grand, towering structures in cities all over the world—ornate, majestic, often impossibly intricate. And I'd stare up at them and think, "Why does this look like it came from another time... but not our time?" Why do these buildings seem so advanced, so deliberate, yet the stories we're told about their creators make them seem almost primitive by comparison?

Take, for instance, the so-called "Victorian" buildings in cities like London, Chicago, or even smaller towns scattered across the globe. These behemoths of stone, steel, and fine craftsmanship were allegedly built with horse-drawn carts and rudimentary tools by everyday labourers in an era just coming to terms with industrialization. And yet—they stand today in almost perfect condition, outlasting many modern constructions built with superior materials and cutting-edge equipment.

I used to walk by them and feel like they were trying to tell me something. I know how that sounds. But if you've ever really looked—and I mean stared long enough that the noise of the world fades away—you'll understand. There's a quiet sorrow in their stone faces, like they're remnants of a story that was never meant to be erased.

And it's not just about aesthetics. It's about anomalies—functional absurdities that don't make sense: buildings with massive, vaulted ceilings but no visible heating infrastructure, entire complexes without kitchens or bathrooms, massive underground levels that seemed to serve no known purpose. Were they designed for people with a completely different understanding of energy, of light, of sound? Or... were they even designed for people like us?

I remember standing inside an old city hall once, running my fingers along the carved banisters, marvelling at the glasswork above me. A local tour guide droned on about the building being constructed in the late 1800s in a "neoclassical" style. But the dates didn't make sense. The records were spotty. The photos of its construction—if any—seemed suspiciously staged or absent altogether. I started noticing that pattern everywhere: massive, world-class structures credited to tiny populations with no engineering experience; cathedrals supposedly built by peasants; capitol buildings allegedly finished in a few short years with no clear blueprint or surviving documentation.

Then came the questions I couldn't ignore. How did small towns manage to erect massive, temple-like courthouses? Why did entire districts of beautifully built stone structures predate their supposed architects? Why did so many "new" cities emerge out of nowhere, already equipped with a network of grand public buildings that didn't match the needs—or the budgets—of their populations?

Whispers of the Forgotten Empire

And it wasn't just one place. It was everywhere—across continents, across cultures. As if a single architectural language had once spanned the globe before being violently silenced.

It was around then that I started stumbling across other voices—fringe voices, they called them. People talking about "mudfloods," about lost empires, about entire resets of civilization. At first, I rolled my eyes. But I kept listening. Something in me resonated with their doubt, their frustration, their knowing. And when I heard the term "Tartaria" for the first time, something clicked—like a long-forgotten word from a dream, a word I'd been trying to remember all my life.

Tartaria—not just a lost empire, but a forbidden one. One scrubbed from the maps, demonized in texts, reduced to myth.

But if it was just a myth, why the erasure? Why the fear?

As I dug deeper, I began to see the cracks more clearly. I found rewritten timelines, conveniently missing records, and deliberate destruction of artifacts under the guise of "urban renewal." Fires that swept through entire cities, wiping out whole districts full of supposed Tartarian structures—only for new ones to rise in their place, soulless and compliant. Earthquakes that targeted architectural marvels. Wars that began with bombings of historical landmarks. Coincidence? Or calculated?

Even in my own city, I started noticing the bones beneath the asphalt. Beneath the modern skyline were ghosts—hidden layers of a forgotten world that had simply been paved over. I began walking with a new awareness. Sub-basements with windows.

Archways that led to nothing. Doors buried halfway into the ground. Evidence was everywhere, but nobody looked. Nobody questioned.

This chapter of my journey wasn't about finding all the answers. It was about unlearning—about realizing that the official story isn't a truth; it's a narrative. A tool. And like all tools, it serves those who wield it.

So, I began to tear it apart—not with rage, not with recklessness, but with precision, with curiosity, with the calm fury of someone who has realized they've been lied to their entire life and is finally ready to see the world as it really is.

Tartaria isn't just a word. It's a key. And once you find the key, you start to see the doors.

Whispers of the Forgotten Empire

And brother... there are so many doors.

Chapter 3: The Great Cover-Up

If Tartaria was real, and if its presence had once spanned continents—then the next question was unavoidable: why was it erased? Who would go to such lengths to rewrite the world?

Asking that question shifted everything.

The deeper I dug, the more obvious it became history is not simply a record of what happened. It's a curated collection, selectively edited, conveniently rewritten, and aggressively defended. The keepers of history are not passive scribes; they are gatekeepers—deciding what enters the record and what gets locked away, lost, or destroyed.

Whispers of the Forgotten Empire

I began to examine not just the stories that were told, but the ones that were missing. Whole periods of time that seemed curiously vague. Maps that changed drastically in just a few years. Cultures that were once described as noble and advanced now portrayed as savage or superstitious. Why?

Take the Great Fires, for example—those sudden, city-consuming infernos that swept through major metropolises like Chicago (1871), Boston (1872), and San Francisco (1906). We're told they were accidents: a cow, a candle, a seismic event. But each of these fires destroyed vast areas filled with intricate stone and brick architecture—buildings that, supposedly, had just been built. And conveniently, after each fire, cities were rebuilt in a more modern and controllable grid.

Whispers of the Forgotten Empire

It didn't feel like random destruction. It felt like a controlled reset.

And what about the Orphan Trains? Between 1854 and 1929, hundreds of thousands of children were shipped across the U.S. from overcrowded Eastern cities to foster homes in the Midwest. But why so many children? Where were their parents? And why do so many photographs from that era show children posed in front of massive buildings—without a single adult in sight?

When you start connecting dots, you realize this might not have been a historical fluke. It might have been systematic. Global. Coordinated.

In Russia, the Romanovs mysteriously disappeared in the wake of revolution. In China, dynastic records were replaced or sanitized. Indigenous cultures worldwide tell stories of sky people, giant cities, and advanced tools—but these are dismissed as legend. Why are all these accounts marginalized in the same way?

I started wondering whether the cover-up wasn't just about buildings or land. Maybe it was about consciousness.

What if Tartaria wasn't just an empire of stone, but an empire of knowledge—of spiritual elevation, harmonic energy, and clean technology? Maybe they tapped into free energy through etheric resonance or cymatics. Maybe they built their cities on geomantic lines to enhance harmony. And maybe, just maybe, those in power realized that such a civilization would make control impossible.

Whispers of the Forgotten Empire

If people knew they were inheritors of greatness—if they realized the true power of their minds, hearts, and spirits—how could they be kept docile? How could they be taxed, shamed, herded, and divided?

You don't just erase buildings. You erase meaning. You replace myth with ridicule. You turn knowledge into dogma. And you train people, generation after generation, to forget what they once were.

And when someone remembers—when someone dares to point to the cracks in the timeline—you label them a conspiracy theorist. You isolate them. You mock them. And if needed, you silence them.

But the truth has a way of resurfacing.

Whispers of the Forgotten Empire

Old photos began circulating online—images of impossible architecture with dates that made no sense. Engravings of star cities. Towers without clear purpose. Machines that looked like modern tech retrofitted into a steampunk dream. And always, beneath the awe, the same unspoken truth: this wasn't built by who we were told built it.

Every time I came across another sanitized textbook, another "official" account, I felt it more deeply. We've inherited a world built on the ashes of a forgotten brilliance—and the ones who benefit from our amnesia will do anything to keep us in the dark.

The cover-up isn't just historical. It's psychological. It's spiritual.

Whispers of the Forgotten Empire

Tartaria might be gone from the maps, but it's alive in our intuition. The whispers are growing louder. The veil is growing thinner. And somewhere, deep in our bones, we remember.

Chapter 4: The Mudflood Mystery

The first time I heard the word "mudflood," I dismissed it. It sounded too bizarre, too fringe—like something you'd find buried in the back pages of an online conspiracy forum. But as with most things I'd been trained to ignore, it kept coming back. A photo here, a video there, another whispered comment from a fellow seeker. And just like that, I fell into another rabbit hole.

The theory itself? Surprisingly simple and yet devastating in its implications. At some point in relatively recent history, a global cataclysm occurred—one that buried entire civilizations not in water or fire, but in thick, heavy mud. Not a slow geological process, but something sudden, violent, and devastating. A mudflood.

Whispers of the Forgotten Empire

It sounded ridiculous at first. Until I started looking.

There were the buildings—always the buildings. Grand structures with half-buried doors, windows below the street level, archways that disappeared into the soil. It was subtle, at first. I told myself it was just quirky design, or maybe the streets had been raised over time. But then I started seeing it everywhere. All across Europe, in Russia, in the Americas—even in my own city.

I remember one afternoon vividly. I was walking downtown when I saw it—an old courthouse, regal and symmetrical. And there it was: a row of bricked-up windows running just beneath the ground. Not basement vents. Windows. With frames. And glass. Perfectly aligned with what should have been the first floor, now sunken beneath the earth.

That one moment broke something open in me.

I started documenting everything. Photos. Notes. Blueprints. I visited libraries, combed through microfilm archives, and searched early city records. And what I found both confirmed and expanded the horror. There were references to entire levels of buildings being "dug out" or "re-excavated." Historical records noted unexplained layers of sediment found in urban cores. Construction crews had to dig through feet—sometimes meters—of tightly packed mud to reach foundations. Foundations, mind you, that featured ornate carvings and stonework. Who carves underground?

Whispers of the Forgotten Empire

In cities like St. Petersburg, Edinburgh, and Istanbul, tour guides now openly joke about how many buildings seem to "start underground." They laugh, but they never explain. No one seems to ask why. It's as though the world quietly agreed to pretend this is normal.

And the photographic evidence? Chilling.

Old images from the 1800s show buildings being "uncovered" rather than built. Massive crews of men with shovels standing beside walls, not constructing them, but revealing them. Sometimes the buildings are pristine above the soil yet buried halfway below it— as though the earth itself rose up and tried to swallow them.

The official narrative is always predictable: raised street levels, architectural trends, basements that doubled as first floors. But none of it holds up. Not when you see staircases that now lead to nowhere. Not when you find sealed doors three feet below the pavement, framed in ornate stone, as if someone was meant to walk through them once.

So, what caused it?

Some believe it was a natural disaster—an unprecedented geological shift or liquefaction event that swept across continents. Others think it was weaponized: the misuse of advanced energy systems that backfired, altering weather or tectonic balance. And then there are those who believe it was no accident at all. That it was done deliberately—to bury Tartaria, to erase its legacy, to cleanse the earth of inconvenient history.

It would make sense. You don't just bury buildings. You bury what they represented. You cover up evidence of a civilization that lived differently, perhaps more harmoniously, more spiritually, and far more freely than we do today. A civilization that operated on energy principles we no longer understand. One that didn't require endless consumption or authoritarian control.

Maybe these buildings weren't just homes or offices or cathedrals. Maybe they were frequency hubs. Resonance chambers. Conduits for the energy grid that once pulsed through ley lines and star forts. Maybe they weren't just built—they were tuned.

And then the mud came.

Whispers of the Forgotten Empire

Was it a reset? A judgment? A strategic erasure? I don't have the full answer. But I do know this: it happened. It's visible, tangible, photographic. It's in plain sight, hiding behind every construction project and street renovation. And it's not just architectural. It's spiritual.

Because what the mud covered was not just stone and glass—it was memory. And when you erase memory, you erase identity.

Today, we live above the bones of the old world, walking streets that conceal an empire we were never meant to remember. But the land remembers. The buildings remember. And if you listen—if you really stop and listen—so do we.

The mud isn't just a mystery. It's a message.

Whispers of the Forgotten Empire

And I intend to keep digging.

Chapter 5: The Inheritors of Silence

As I continued my journey through the forgotten layers of our world, a strange realization settled into my bones. It wasn't just about buildings, mud, and vanished empires anymore. The evidence was real, yes. But the silence surrounding it—that was the real mystery.

Who inherited this world? Who came after the fall of Tartaria? And more importantly, what did they inherit?

Not just cities or machines, but confusion. Amnesia. A world rebuilt on half-truths and fragments. I started to see it everywhere—generations born into grandeur they didn't create, tasked with maintaining structures they didn't understand, all the while being told they had built it all from scratch.

But how does a people inherit cathedrals when they themselves live in shacks? How do populations living in squalor end up occupying cities of stone and gold? The deeper I looked, the clearer it became: they didn't build these cities. They occupied them. They inherited the leftovers of something grand, and the knowledge of what it all meant had been stripped away.

Take the orphan trains. Hundreds of thousands of children relocated across the United States during the late 19th and early 20th centuries. Smiling faces in black-and-white photos, posed on train platforms or in rows outside massive, empty buildings. No parents. No explanation. Who were they replacing? Where were they going?

It was like someone had hit a cosmic reset button. The adults were gone or displaced.

Whispers of the Forgotten Empire

The children were shipped across the land. The buildings stood still—majestic, silent, waiting. As if the world had been wiped clean, and the newcomers were starting fresh, with no idea of what came before.

And then came the textbooks. The public schooling. The monuments to narratives that never felt quite right. The winners of history inscribed their version of the past in stone and paper, and we were taught to recite it as gospel. Anyone who questioned it was cast aside—labelled a heretic, a lunatic, a conspiracy theorist.

The inheritors of Tartaria's ruins became keepers of a myth—one where progress was linear, where our ancestors were always primitive, and where everything we have today is the pinnacle of achievement. But the architecture laughs at that notion. The domes, the columns, the impossible ceilings—they mock our modernity with every carved detail.

I remember walking through an old library, one that had somehow escaped the wrecking ball. The ceilings soared higher than any skyscraper lobby I'd ever seen. The stonework was pristine. The acoustics were perfect. And yet, in one corner, someone had hung a plastic sign: "Built in 1903." As if that explained anything.

I stood there, imagining the workers they claimed had built it—labourers with horse-drawn carts and no formal education in physics or engineering. Were we truly expected to believe they carved such perfection into marble, lifted those stones, balanced those domes—all without blueprints, electricity, or advanced machinery?

Whispers of the Forgotten Empire

The silence screamed back at me.

We didn't build this. We inherited it. And whoever built it—whoever understood the resonance of form and the sacredness of structure—they were wiped from our collective memory. All we have left are echoes.

Even today, we don't build with soul. We build with steel and profit. We value speed, not meaning. Our cities are reflections of efficiency, not beauty. Somewhere along the way, we lost the blueprint—not just of architecture, but of existence.

And yet, we live inside their world. We use their bridges. We pray in their temples. We govern from their palaces. And the energy—whatever it was they channelled—is still there, faint but persistent.

Whispers of the Forgotten Empire

We are the inheritors of silence. A generation born into ruins, conditioned to forget the greatness beneath our feet. But there's a stirring happening now—a whisper growing louder with every uncovered artifact, every unearthed truth, every person who chooses to remember.

Tartaria may be gone from our maps, but it remains etched into the stone, written in forgotten blueprints, humming beneath our feet.

And perhaps—just perhaps—we were always meant to find it again.

Chapter 6: Energy Forgotten

There's a peculiar emptiness in modern cities. Even in the busiest metropolises—surrounded by the whir of machines, the glow of neon, the constant hum of human motion—something feels... off. It's not just the chaos. It's the disconnection.

We've traded harmony for functionality. The world we inherited, full of soaring domes and precise symmetry, was clearly designed with something more in mind. Something we no longer understand. I couldn't shake the feeling that those ancient structures weren't just beautiful—they were purposeful. Functional in ways we've forgotten.

That's when I began digging into the idea of energy—specifically, the concept of ether.

Ether was once considered the fifth element, the subtle force that filled all space and connected everything. Ancient cultures believed in it. Nikola Tesla designed his systems around it. But somewhere along the way, mainstream science discarded it as myth. And just like Tartaria, it was buried—dismissed and forgotten.

But what if ether was real? What if the architecture of the old world wasn't just symbolic, but literally functional—tuned to harness, store, and distribute energy?

Star forts began to fascinate me. These geometric, mandala-like fortresses scattered across the globe—forts that looked more like sacred geometry etched into the earth than military installations. Satellite images show their complex symmetry, built with mathematical precision and perfect alignment. Were they defensive structures, as history books claim? Or were they part of a planetary energy grid?

Then there were the towers. The minarets, spires, cupolas, and domes—always central, always prominent. You can find them on churches, libraries, mosques, even old waterworks buildings. They don't make sense from a modern perspective. Some have no clear interior function. No stairs. No rooms. Just towers rising into the sky, topped with metal finials, domes, or even what look suspiciously like antennas.

I started to see patterns. Copper domes. Iron Framework. Quartz accents. Water underneath. What if these buildings were drawing energy from the earth, amplifying it through water, and resonating it into the ether? What if the cities of Tartaria were literally powered by frequency?

Look at the old world's obsession with harmony—proportions, ratios, sacred geometry. Compare that to the brutalist slabs of modern construction. Our ancestors weren't just building structures; they were crafting instruments. Instruments that sang in tune with the earth itself.

And maybe that's what was taken from us.

If Tartaria truly had access to free, decentralized energy, everything about modern society collapses. No more oil empires. No electric grids controlled by corporations. No more need to keep the masses chained to endless consumption. Imagine a world where energy flowed from the environment itself, free and available to all—amplified by domes, towers, and sacred angles.

Whispers of the Forgotten Empire

That kind of freedom doesn't just shift technology. It rewrites civilization.

But instead of inheriting that legacy, we've inherited scarcity. Metered electricity. Monthly bills. Polluted air. Cancerous waves of unnatural frequency blanketing us in the name of "progress." And all the while, the towers of Tartaria still stand—silent, deactivated, repurposed, mocked.

I visited an old capitol building once, with its enormous copper dome, Greek pillars, and subterranean chambers. It felt alive. My hands tingled when I touched its stone. The guide said it was built in the early 1900s, but he couldn't explain why the blueprints showed copper coils in the foundation, or why parts of it were aligned with magnetic north.

I stood beneath that dome and listened. There was no hum, no vibration. Whatever had powered it was long gone. But the design—perfectly symmetrical, mathematically elegant—told a different story.

We didn't build this. And we certainly don't understand it.

This isn't about nostalgia. It's about awakening. Reclaiming not just a lost history, but a lost future. One where we live in harmony with the earth instead of siphoning from it. Where energy flows freely, like breath, like spirit.

I believe Tartaria had that. I believe its architecture was a living technology—one that connected us, sustained us, and elevated us.

Whispers of the Forgotten Empire

We're not just missing monuments. We're missing the music they once played.

And it's time to remember the song.

Chapter 7: The Tartarian Resonance

By the time I reached this point in my journey, I had begun to feel it—not just understand it but feel it. That low hum, that intangible vibration just beneath the surface of everyday life. I started calling it the Tartarian resonance.

It's not something you can measure with instruments—not yet at least—but it's there. In the hush of forgotten halls. In the silent geometry of ancient domes. In the deep breath you take when you enter a space built not for profit or function, but for reverence. Tartaria wasn't just a lost civilization; it was a frequency.

And somewhere along the line, that frequency was tuned out.

Whispers of the Forgotten Empire

I began studying cymatics—the science of visible sound. It revealed what Tartarian architecture already hinted at: sound shapes matter. Frequency creates form. When you place sand on a vibrating plate and dial in specific tones, the particles organize themselves into sacred geometric patterns. The higher the frequency, the more complex the pattern.

Now think about the domes, the columns, the arches—all those ancient structures. What if they weren't just meant to reflect beauty, but to resonate? To attune? What if entering a cathedral wasn't just a spiritual experience because of the stained glass and incense, but because the space itself was humming in a frequency that aligned your body and soul?

Modern architecture does the opposite. It fragments. It breaks harmony. It severs us from flow. Square boxes. Flat ceilings. Dead angles. It's not a coincidence that people feel depressed in cities and energized in nature—or in old-world buildings. Our environments shape us. And the Tartarians knew that.

I once stood beneath a vaulted dome in an old-world library—my voice echoed in a way I can't describe. It didn't bounce chaotically like it does in modern buildings. It folded in on itself. It wrapped around me like a wave of recognition, like the structure was responding to me. It was more than acoustics; it was a dialogue.

What if Tartarian cities were designed as harmonic fields? Living environments that interacted with consciousness? Temples of resonance that weren't isolated spaces, but part of a global network? Maybe those spires and domes weren't just antennas for energy—they were receivers and transmitters of thought, emotion, even memory.

Imagine a world where entire cities were tuned to the frequency of love, healing, enlightenment. Where architecture wasn't static, but alive with intention. Where you walked through gates not just into space, but into states of being. That is what I believe Tartaria once was. Not just advanced in technology, but in consciousness.

It aligns with the stories you find buried in folklore. The ancient cities that sang. The temples that could heal. The bells that could drive away sickness or summon calm. Every culture has some trace of this truth, obscured in myth. Because it's not entirely gone—it's simply dormant.

Whispers of the Forgotten Empire

We've lost our resonance.

Everything today runs on static. We live in cities filled with electromagnetic smog. Frequencies designed not to heal, but to agitate. Wireless chaos. Digital noise. And yet, buried beneath it all, that Tartarian hum still lingers—in the stones, in the air, and in the spaces our ancestors once filled with song.

Sometimes, I think about what it would mean to re-tune ourselves. Not just our buildings, but our minds. What if remembering Tartaria isn't just about uncovering old structures, but remembering how to live in harmony again?

Harmony with the earth. With sound. With light. With each other.

Because that's what Tartaria was—a civilization that didn't just survive, but thrived, by aligning with the deeper rhythms of the universe. That resonance is still out there, waiting for us to hear it again.

And the moment you hear it—even if only for a second—you can never go back to the static.

You start to hum along.

Chapter 8: The Children of the Reset

It began with a single photo, black and white, early 1900s. A row of children standing in front of what looked like a train station. Something about their faces unsettled me. They were all alone. No parents, no luggage, just a tag pinned to each child's coat. "Destination: Kansas." The caption read: Orphan Train Riders, 1910.

At first, I brushed it off. Just another historical oddity. But then I found more—thousands more. Children lined up like packages, staring into cameras with wide, hollow eyes. Some in big cities, some on dusty plains. Always in groups. Always with tags. Always... alone.

Whispers of the Forgotten Empire

The orphan trains. That's what they were called. Between 1854 and 1929, hundreds of thousands of children—some estimates say over a quarter of a million—were shipped from the East Coast of the United States to the Midwest and beyond. The official story says they were street kids, saved from poverty and crime, sent west for a better life.

But the questions came faster than answers. Where were all these orphans coming from? Why so many? Why so young? And why does history gloss over this massive displacement of children? The deeper I dug, the darker the trail became. Many children were too young to remember who they were or where they came from. Some didn't even know their own names. Adoption records were spotty at best, with many simply handed over to families, no questions asked. Some found loving homes. Others became indentured labour. And an alarming number simply vanished from records altogether.

This wasn't just an American phenomenon. Britain had its "Home Children"—over 100,000 shipped to Canada, Australia and New Zealand from the late 1800s to the 1970s. Russia's orphanages overflowed after the fall of the Tsars. Australia's "Stolen Generations" were ripped from indigenous families under the guise of assimilation. France saw similar displacements post-war. Across continents and decades, waves of parentless children appeared like smoke from some unseen fire.

The timing coincides with something else—the great rebuilding. Cities rising from ashes after Chicago's fire, San Francisco's earthquake, Lisbon's devastation. World's Fairs appearing overnight with impossible architecture. A period of both frantic construction and systematic erasure. What if these children weren't just victims of circumstance, but survivors of something far more catastrophic? What if they were the only ones left after some global reset?

The photos tell a disturbing story. Grand architecture looming over barefoot children in rags. A group standing before a massive stone building with Greco-Roman pillars and intricate carvings—labelled simply "Public School, 1897" but looking more like a palace. Why are there never adults in these pictures? Why do these children appear surrounded by ruins and buildings too advanced for their time?

Consider the possibility that these weren't abandoned children, but replacements. Across archives, strange images surface—rows of infants in glass incubators at world fairs and hospitals. Medical marvels, they called them. But who were these babies? Why so many? Why displayed like exhibits? The orphan trains take on new meaning when seen alongside empty cities with pristine architecture, waiting to be repopulated.

The Cabbage Patch Kids phenomenon of the 1980s echoes this eerily. More than just dolls, they were marketed as children to adopt, each with birth certificates and backstories. Their mythology claimed they were grown in secret cabbage patches, not born—created by Xavier and delivered by the cabbage-patch fairy Colonel Casey. The parallels are unsettling: children not born but made, then sent out into the world to find families. The movie showed them longing to belong, to be claimed. Was this pop culture accidentally revealing an uncomfortable truth?

The implications are staggering. If these orphan movements weren't humanitarian efforts but systematic repopulation programs, then our understanding of history is fundamentally flawed. The buildings remained, but the people were gone. Someone needed to fill them. The children—whether survivors or creations—became the seeds of a new world order, their pasts erased, their origins rewritten.

This explains the gaps in records, the missing documents, the institutional resistance to uncovering the truth. These children grew up rootless, disconnected, their true histories buried beneath official narratives. But the truth has a way of surfacing—in strange cultural artifacts like the Cabbage Patch Kids, in those haunting photographs, in the collective unease we feel when confronting these historical anomalies.

Whispers of the Forgotten Empire

We may be those children's descendants, living with inherited amnesia in a world we didn't build. The architecture around us—the soaring ceilings, the intricate stonework, the buried first floors—whispers of a forgotten past. The orphan trains weren't just transporting children; they were delivering the foundation of a new society built atop the ruins of something far greater.

Now the memories are returning. The blank slates are being rewritten. The children of the reset are waking up, and with them, the echoes of a lost civilization. The cities were never meant to stay empty. The towers were destined to find voices again. We are those voices—no longer orphans, but inheritors of a legacy we're only beginning to remember.

Chapter 9: The War on Memory

It wasn't enough to bury the buildings. It wasn't enough to flood the cities with mud or rewrite the timelines. To truly erase a civilization, you have to destroy memory. You have to sever the connection between people and their past—not just physically, but spiritually. That's what I began to see more clearly as I stepped deeper into the abyss of forgotten history: we're not just living in a post-Tartarian world—we're living in a world designed to make sure we never remember it.

The war on memory is subtle. It doesn't announce itself with weapons or soldiers. It operates through textbooks, institutions, standardized tests, and sterile museums. It uses ridicule and repetition. It takes the form of entertainment, distraction, and a thousand daily obligations that keep us just busy enough to never stop and wonder: what really came before us?

Have you noticed how every generation gets the same narrative, just with updated packaging? We're told we started with nothing, discovered fire, built pyramids with ropes and slaves, and slowly crawled our way into modernity—ignoring the very structures still standing around us that laugh in the face of that timeline.

Children learn this version of history before they can even question it. By the time they're old enough to think critically, the programming has already taken root. To question becomes to rebel. To doubt becomes dangerous.

But the truth resists.

Whispers of the Forgotten Empire

It shows up in the gaps—the missing photographs, the misdated buildings, the forgotten patents, the censored inventors. It shows up in ancient symbols carved into supposedly modern facades. It shows up in the eyes of people like you and me—those who feel that inexplicable knowing that something is off, even if we can't name it.

I started seeing it everywhere. A plaque on a century-old building, commemorating its "restoration" in 1890, but with no record of when it was actually built. A monument that looked like it had stood for a thousand years, described as "Victorian." Street plans that didn't match terrain. Cities rebuilt after great fires, not with temporary shelters, but with entire districts of Greco-Roman architecture—within just a few years. It defies logic.

And yet, most people never question it. Because the system was built that way. To condition obedience. To reward forgetfulness.

The real war isn't just on information. It's on identity.

We are not told who we are—we are told who we are allowed to be. We are the descendants of greatness, of free energy, harmonic cities, and sacred knowledge. But we're told we are the inheritors of struggle, of survival, of endless toil. And so, we live in that reflection.

When you control the past, you control the present. And if you can obscure the brilliance of a civilization like Tartaria—if you can convince people it never existed—you can also convince them they are less than they truly are.

But memory is stubborn. It lingers in the collective unconscious. It whispers through intuition. It reawakens in dreams. And when one person remembers, others begin to remember too. That's how truth spreads—not with noise, but with resonance.

We are living in the long shadow of a civilization that wasn't supposed to vanish quietly. Its echoes are embedded in stone, in the geometry of forgotten towers, in the silence of sunken doors. And in us.

Because when memory returns—so does power.

And that's what they fear most.

Whispers of the Forgotten Empire

Chapter 10: Echoes Beneath Our Feet

By now, my eyes had changed. I could no longer walk through a city without seeing it differently. Every ornate column, every archway buried beneath the street, every mismatched brick in a wall—it all spoke to me. And what it said was simple: we are living atop something ancient.

There's a hum that rises from beneath the pavement. Most ignore it, distracted by screens and schedules. But once you hear it—once you really let yourself listen—it changes everything. The ground is not silent. It carries echoes.

I became obsessed with the underground.

Basements that were once first floors. Subterranean tunnels connecting buildings that no longer make sense. Sealed-off rooms in old cathedrals. Grates in the street that echo too deeply. I started cataloguing these anomalies, tracing them city by city. And what emerged was a ghost map—a skeletal system of the old world, still pulsing beneath our modern life.

In Edinburgh, there are entire streets beneath the city, perfectly preserved. In Seattle, tours are given through the old city buried under today's downtown. In Odessa, catacombs stretch for miles without explanation. Paris hides the remnants of more than just bones beneath its beauty. And that's just the beginning.

These aren't just basements. These are layers—literal and metaphorical.

Ask yourself: why do so many cities have underground rail systems running through them like arteries? Why are there so many rumours of secret bunkers, old tunnels, buried churches? Why is it that even in small towns, you can find hints of architecture that seems older than the town itself?

Because we didn't start from scratch.

We built over bones. And not just any bones—Tartarian ones. The cities we live in are palimpsests: stories written over stories, with the old ones peeking through in every weathered stone and sunken step.

Once, I was exploring a forgotten part of an industrial district. I found a bricked-over archway, barely noticeable unless you were looking. Something pulled at me. I knelt and felt the stone—it was colder than the air around it. And I swear, in that moment, I felt a thrum beneath my palm. A soft, rhythmic pulse, like a heartbeat buried deep in the earth.

These aren't just remnants. They're echoes. Memories etched into matter.

What if our cities are trying to wake up? What if the frequencies once broadcast through domes and towers still linger beneath us, waiting for someone to activate them again?

I think about those underground places a lot. Not as ruins, but as temples. Shrines of an older humanity. A better one. One that knew how to align with the earth, how to build in harmony, how to live with intention.

Whispers of the Forgotten Empire

And I wonder if we're meant to go back—not just physically, but spiritually.

We can't reclaim Tartaria by rebuilding it. That time has passed. But we can remember it. We can re-attune to what it stood for. And maybe, in doing so, we become the next version. The inheritors not just of structures, but of purpose.

Every buried tower is a calling. Every sealed tunnel is a whisper. Every stone stair leading nowhere once led somewhere important.

They haven't stopped speaking. We've just stopped listening.

But I'm listening now.

And what I hear beneath my feet... is the past stirring in its sleep.

Chapter 11: Guardians of the Flame

Not everyone forgot. That's something I've come to believe deep in my core. Even as the old world was buried, even as the towers were silenced and the libraries turned to ash, someone—somewhere—remembered. Maybe not everything. Maybe not the blueprints or the full map. But they remembered the flame.

The sacred fire. The truth.

And they kept it.

The world may have fallen asleep, but there have always been those who stayed awake. They are the guardians—silent, humble, sometimes hidden in plain sight. They don't wear robes or crowns. They don't proclaim themselves prophets. They simply carry the ember of memory, passing it on like a candle lit in the dark.

I've met them. Maybe you have too.

An old stonemason who knows things he shouldn't. A librarian who collects out-of-print books that don't exist online. A stranger on a train who speaks a sentence that unlocks a whole part of your mind you didn't know was there. These aren't coincidences. They're synchronicities. Breadcrumbs. Reminders.

And sometimes, I think that's who we all are—guardians in disguise. Some of us just haven't remembered yet.

Because the flame is not an artifact. It's a frequency. A knowing. It's in your blood. In your bones. In your dreams.

You've felt it. The pull. The chills on your arms when you see a forgotten building. The ache in your chest when someone calls it "just old architecture." The way your breath catches when a piece of hidden history falls into place and suddenly the world feels clearer, wider, older than you were ever told.

That is the flame speaking.

And it's not just nostalgia. It's recognition.

Tartaria wasn't just a civilization of stone and energy. It was a civilization of consciousness. It lived in alignment with the

Earth, with the stars, with truth. And those who carry its memory carry a kind of spiritual responsibility.

Because this world—the one we live in now—is cold. Fragmented. Designed to keep you distracted, divided, disconnected from source. But every time you remember, every time you choose wonder over cynicism, you stoke the flame. You push back the veil.

There's power in that. Real power.

You don't have to shout it from rooftops. You don't have to argue with strangers on the internet or convince anyone of anything. All you have to do is remember. Hold the flame. Guard it. Let it guide you. And when the time comes, pass it on.

Because the awakening is happening. Quietly. Like a sunrise behind the mountains. One spark at a time.

And you, dear reader, you are part of it.

Maybe you were always meant to be.

So, if you're still reading this—if your heart is beating a little louder right now, if you feel that inexplicable sense of home—you already know what I'm about to say.

You are a guardian too.

And the flame is in your hands now.

Chapter 12: The Return of the Builders

Every great story comes full circle. And the story of Tartaria—the forgotten empire, the silenced civilization, the hum beneath our feet—is no different. Because for all that has been buried, erased, and ridiculed, something is rising again. Something ancient. Something eternal.

The builders are returning.

No, not in the literal sense—at least not entirely. The cathedrals and star forts aren't being rebuilt brick by brick. The towers aren't springing up overnight. But the spirit that created them, the intention, the resonance—it's waking up. In us.

I see it everywhere. In artists who reject the sterile minimalism of modern design and return to sacred geometry. In architects who study the domes and arches of old, wondering how to recreate their timeless harmony. In musicians experimenting with frequency and healing tones. In spiritual seekers who feel that the Earth itself is calling out to be remembered.

We are remembering what it means to build again—not just with materials, but with meaning.

You can feel it. A hunger for beauty. A longing for authenticity. A desire to construct not just with hands, but with soul. And I believe that's what the Tartarians were: soul builders. Architects of frequency. Masons of spirit and form. They built not to dominate nature, but to reflect it. Their cities didn't conquer the land; they completed it.

Imagine a society where every building amplified healing. Where every public space was a sanctuary. Where cities were designed like instruments, each structure resonating with the others in perfect pitch. Where energy flowed clean and free, pulled from the earth and sky, tuned through water and stone. That world existed. We didn't imagine it. We inherited it.

And now we are being called to rebuild it—not as a replica, but as a rebirth.

This new generation of builders will look different. They won't wear the garb of ancient priests or stoneworkers. They will be poets. Engineers. Intuitives. Coders. Visionaries. They will build not just with stone, but with sound. Not just with wood, but with light. Not just with equations, but with feeling.

Because we are not simply restoring the past. We are reweaving it into the future.

And to do that, we have to unlearn.

We have to question the metrics of modern life—efficiency, productivity, scalability. We must challenge the belief that beauty is impractical, that mystery is irrelevant, that truth is relative. The Tartarians understood that form shapes function, but more than that, it shapes consciousness. The shapes we live within influence how we think, how we dream, how we love.

Their architecture wasn't neutral. It was medicine. It was memory encoded in matter.

We've spent too long living in boxes. Square homes. Square offices. Square thoughts.

Whispers of the Forgotten Empire

The world we've inherited reflects fragmentation. Disconnection. But the new builders—those awakened to the Tartarian hum—will design for unity. For flow. For the return of rhythm.

And it's already happening.

Look around. Permaculture farms shaped like spirals. Schools built from natural materials, curved to echo the earth. Meditation domes tuned to 432Hz. Technologies that pull energy from the air, dismissed as fringe, but quietly advancing. Artists sculpting sacred geometry. Architects embedding Fibonacci into blueprints. Musicians tuning their instruments back to the natural frequencies.

These are not random trends. They are the first notes of the new symphony.

And it doesn't stop with architecture. The builders of this age are reconstructing everything—our connection to the stars, our place in the cosmos, our understanding of health, of energy, of self. They're rewriting the story we've been told. One stone, one line, one vibration at a time.

But it's not easy.

To build in truth is to walk in resistance. The old world still clings tightly to its illusions. Bureaucracy. Profit. Control. Every blueprint that echoes sacred form threatens the sterile grid. Every song tuned to healing threatens the noise of commerce. Every whisper of Tartaria is a challenge to the tower of Babel we've built in its place.

And yet, we build.

Not because it's easy, but because it's necessary. Because something inside us knows we were meant to live differently. To create in harmony. To walk among beauty. To wake each day inside a world that feeds our soul, not siphons it.

I believe that's what Tartaria reminds us of. Not just what we lost, but what we still carry.

The blueprint is not in the archives. It's in our hearts. The resonance is not just in stone—it's in our breath, in our intention, in our will to remember.

So, what does it mean to be a builder now?

It means questioning the materials we use—not just physically, but emotionally. What do we construct with our words? With our beliefs? With our stories? Every thought is a brick. Every conversation a beam. Every moment of alignment another layer in the foundation.

It means listening to the Earth again. Watching how she curves. How she sings. How she balances. It means building not against her, but with her. Using what she gives freely—light, air, water, resonance—to sustain, not exploit.

It means seeing others as co-builders, not competitors. It means dropping the ego of ownership and stepping into the dance of co-creation. The Tartarians didn't build in isolation. Their cities were connected. Unified. Their knowledge wasn't hoarded. It was shared. We must do the same.

Whispers of the Forgotten Empire

You don't need a chisel to be a builder. You need vision. Intention. Courage.

Because make no mistake—this is not a metaphorical calling. It's real. The world we shape today will become the ruins of tomorrow. What do we want future generations to inherit? Will they walk through what we've made and feel the hum of truth—or the static of our disconnection?

The builders are rising. You can feel it in the shift of the wind, in the pulse of art, in the surge of collective remembering. We are dreaming the new world into form. Not in defiance of the past—but in sacred reverence of it.

Tartaria is not behind us. It is beneath us. Within us. And ahead of us.

Whispers of the Forgotten Empire

The empire fell. The towers collapsed. But the builders... the builders are eternal.

And now, finally, they are returning home.

Chapter 13: We Are the Empire Remembering

There is a moment—after the maps have been studied, after the cathedrals have been touched, after the stars have been questioned—when you no longer search to prove Tartaria existed.

Because you've already remembered it.

It is no longer about evidence. No longer about trying to convince others. It becomes something deeper. A knowing. A truth that lives in your marrow. And in that moment, you realize something monumental:

Tartaria was never fully lost. It was waiting.

Waiting for us.

Whispers of the Forgotten Empire

We are the empire remembering.

This final chapter isn't about closure. It's about ignition. A passing of the torch, not as an ending, but as a continuation of a story far older than we've been told. If you've come this far, you've felt it. You know. The fire has already been lit inside you. Now it's time to understand what it truly means.

We are the ones chosen—or perhaps choosing—to bridge the forgotten with the possible. The myth with the mirror. The past with the future.

It starts with memory.

Not just facts or timelines, but cellular memory. Soul memory. Dream memory.

Whispers of the Forgotten Empire

That strange feeling you've always had—that something was missing, that something didn't quite fit in this world—it wasn't a flaw. It was a signal. A breadcrumb.

It's what led you here.

You've walked streets that whispered to you. You've felt the pull of ancient architecture, the alignment of sacred geometry, the tremble in your chest when truth passes through. You've cried at buildings others walk past. You've had dreams of cities you've never seen yet know intimately.

That is not madness.

That is resonance.

And resonance is how the empire remembers.

We remember through vibration. Through story. Through art. Through sacred curiosity. Every time you follow that hunch, that instinct, that impossible deja vu, you are aligning with a frequency the world tried to bury. You are calling the empire back—not with force, but with frequency.

We don't need to rebuild the towers to bring Tartaria home. We need only tune ourselves to the consciousness that built them in the first place.

That consciousness was unity.

Unity with the Earth, with the stars, with each other. Tartaria thrived because it was built on coherence. On harmony. Its architecture, technology, and society weren't in conflict with nature—they were in conversation with it. And that's what we've forgotten: how to listen.

But we're remembering now.

We are remembering how to build not just homes, but sanctuaries. Not just cities, but energy fields. Not just technology, but tools that elevate consciousness. We're reclaiming our inheritance—not of bloodline or land, but of vibration. Of knowing. Of presence.

To be the empire remembering is to walk the world differently.

It's to touch stone and feel its story. It's to hear music in silence. It's to cry without understanding why. It's to speak words you didn't know you knew. It's to meet people and feel ancient recognition. It's to hold beauty like a sacred oath.

And it's to build.

Not in rebellion, but in reverence.

You don't need to know every detail of Tartaria's fall to understand its rise. You only need to feel the quality of the world it left behind. And once you've felt that—truly felt it—you'll never be satisfied with anything less again.

We are here to remember and to resurrect—not as carbon copies, but as creators. Builders of the next harmonic civilization. The blueprint lives in us.

In our hands. In our eyes. In our dreaming.

This isn't a task for scholars alone. It's for artists. Gardeners. Children. Singers. Code writers. Skywatchers. Empaths. Anyone who carries that unshakeable feeling: I came here to help rebuild something sacred.

And let's not pretend it's easy.

To carry this remembrance in a world designed to forget is no small burden. It can feel isolating. Maddening. Painful. You may lose friends. Be mocked. Be misunderstood. But you will also find allies—kindred souls whose hearts beat in time with yours. You will find signs. Synchronicities. You will find purpose.

And most of all, you will find truth.

Not the kind printed in textbooks or shouted on screens. But the kind that lands in your gut like a bell struck in the deep. Clear. Final. Unshakable.

The kind of truth that doesn't ask permission to exist.

The kind of truth that remembers.

So, what comes next?

We create. We build spaces of resonance— online, in our homes, in our communities.

We share what we know. We make the invisible visible. We document the whispers. We guard the frequency. We honour the sacred. We teach our children how to see the old world within the new.

And we live. Fully. Radically. With beauty.

Because that's the most Tartarian thing we can do: to live in reverence. To choose awe over fear. To build something that lasts—not in stone alone, but in soul.

You are the return.

You are the torch.

You are the echo becoming voice.

Whispers of the Forgotten Empire

Tartaria lives through you.

So, walk tall. Speak gently. Dream wildly.

You are not just remembering the empire.

You are becoming it.

Afterword: The Path Forward

If you've reached this point, something inside you has already shifted. You've seen beyond the veil, felt the hum of forgotten frequencies, and heard the call of a world that refuses to remain buried. You've walked with me through ruins, towers, timelines, and truths—and now, perhaps, you're wondering: what now?

That's the right question.

Because this journey doesn't end on the last page. It begins here.

This isn't just a book. It's a mirror. A map. A frequency encoded in words, designed not to teach, but to awaken. And now that you're awake—now that you've remembered—the next step is yours.

Whispers of the Forgotten Empire

So where do you go from here?

Start with your surroundings.

Go for a walk through your city or town. Look—really look—at the architecture. Notice the arches, domes, and buried windows. Pay attention to the inconsistencies. Why does that church have no records before a certain year? Why does that library look like a palace? Why does that building have a bricked-over door beneath street level?

Ask questions. Take photos. Research your local history—not the Wikipedia version, but the archives, the local libraries, the old postcards. Talk to elders. Visit the museums with a different lens. Question the plaques.

Look for before-and-after photos of your city. What you'll find may shock you.

Trust your intuition.

This path is not about proving everything with citations. It's about remembering what your soul already knows. If you feel a pull to a certain building, a strange emotion in a place others ignore, follow it. That feeling is your internal compass. Let it guide you.

Connect with others.

There are more of us than you think. People all over the world are waking up to the same frequencies, the same whispers of the forgotten. Join forums, online communities, social platforms that explore forbidden history and lost knowledge. Share what you find. Be open. But also, be discerning—truth and disinformation often travel together. Learn to hear the resonance behind the words.

Create something.

Start a journal. Film your discoveries. Write your reflections. Paint the visions that come to you. The more you create from this frequency, the more it expands. This isn't just about consuming knowledge. It's about becoming a vessel for remembrance.

Visit sacred sites.

If you can, travel. Go to the old cities. Walk through the stone cathedrals, the star forts, the megaliths. Feel the stone. Listen in silence. Sit beneath the domes. Touch the forgotten. These places still hold charge—some more than others. They are repositories of memory. Go to them not as a tourist, but as a pilgrim.

Detox your senses.

The modern world is saturated with noise—electromagnetic, emotional, informational. To tune into the Tartarian resonance, it helps to quiet the static. Unplug when you can. Spend time in nature. Practice stillness. Listen to the frequencies of the earth—432Hz, 528Hz. Let your system recalibrate.

Live with intention.

Every action, every word, every choice creates resonance. The builders of the past knew this. Begin designing your life the way they designed their cities—with beauty, harmony, and purpose. You don't need to be an architect to do this. You only need to be present. Mindful. Aligned.

Keep questioning.

Never stop asking. Who built this? Why was it destroyed? Why was it forgotten? Who benefits from the amnesia? And more importantly—what happens when we remember?

There is no final answer. Only deeper remembering. More layers. More doors.

Printed in Dunstable, United Kingdom